TECHNICAL
REPORT

The Utilization of Women-Owned Small Businesses in Federal Contracting

Elaine Reardon, Nancy Nicosia,
Nancy Y. Moore

Prepared for the Small Business Administration

RAND
Kauffman-RAND Institute for
Entrepreneurship Public Policy

This study was undertaken in response to a request by the SBA for the RAND Corporation to provide different measures of WOSB representation in federal contracting, by industry. The work was funded by the SBA and completed under the auspices of the RAND Labor and Population program and the Kauffman-RAND Institute for Entrepreneurship Public Policy.

Library of Congress Cataloging-in-Publication Data

Reardon, Elaine.
The utilization of women-owned small businesses in federal contracting / Elaine Reardon, Nancy Nicosia, Nancy Moore.
p. cm.
Includes bibliographical references.
ISBN 978-0-8330-4166-1 (pbk. : alk. paper)
1. Public contracts—United States. 2. Women-owned business enterprises—United States.
I. Nicosia, Nancy. II. Moore, Nancy Y., 1947– III. Title.

HD3861.U6R43 2007
352.5'3082—dc22

2007016169

Published 2007 by the RAND Corporation
1776 Main Street, P.O. Box 2138, Santa Monica, CA 90407-2138
1200 South Hayes Street, Arlington, VA 22202-5050
4570 Fifth Avenue, Suite 600, Pittsburgh, PA 15213-2665
RAND URL: http://www.rand.org/
To order RAND documents or to obtain additional information, contact
Distribution Services: Telephone: (310) 451-7002;
Fax: (310) 451-6915; Email: order@rand.org

Preface

In its procurement efforts, the federal government actively seeks to foster participation by small and disadvantaged businesses. In December 2000, Congress sought to increase procurement from women-owned small businesses (WOSBs) by enacting Section 8(m) of the Small Business Act, 15 U.S.C. Section 637(m), which defines WOSBs as businesses that qualify as "small" according to Small Business Administration (SBA) size standards, are majority-owned by women, and are certified as economically disadvantaged. However, WOSBs need not be economically disadvantaged to qualify for procurement preferences in contracts of up to $3 million ($5 million in manufacturing contracts) in industries where they are found to be "substantially underrepresented."

This study was undertaken in response to a request by the SBA for the RAND Corporation to provide different measures of WOSB representation in federal contracting, by industry. The work was funded by the SBA and completed under the auspices of the RAND Labor and Population program and the Kauffman-RAND Institute for Entrepreneurship Public Policy.

RAND Labor and Population has built an international reputation for conducting objective, high-quality, empirical research to support and improve policies and organizations around the world. Its work focuses on labor markets, social welfare policy, demographic behavior, immigration, international development, and issues related to aging and retirement, with a common aim of understanding how policy and social and economic forces affect individual decisionmaking and the well-being of children, adults, and families.

For more information on RAND Labor and Population, contact Arie Kapteyn, Director, RAND Labor and Population. He can be reached by mail at the RAND Corporation, 1776 Main Street, P.O. Box 2138, Santa Monica, CA 90407-2138; by phone at 310-393-0411, ext. 7973; or by e-mail at Arie_Kapteyn@rand.org.

The Kauffman-RAND Institute for Entrepreneurship Public Policy, which is housed within the RAND Institute for Civil Justice, is dedicated to assessing and improving legal and regulatory policymaking as it relates to small businesses and entrepreneurship in a wide range of settings, including corporate governance, employment law, consumer law, securities regulation, and business ethics. The institute's work is supported by a grant from the Ewing Marion Kauffman Foundation.

For additional information on the RAND Institute for Civil Justice or the Kauffman-RAND Institute for Entrepreneurship Public Policy, please contact Robert T. Reville, Director, RAND Institute for Civil Justice. He can be reached by mail at the RAND Corporation,

1776 Main Street, P.O. Box 2138, Santa Monica, CA 90407–2138; by phone at 310-393-0411, ext. 6786; by Fax at 310-451-6979; or by e-mail at Robert_Reville@rand.org. Information about the RAND Institute for Civil Justice is available at www.rand.org/icj/.

Susan Gates, Director, Kauffman-RAND Institute for Entrepreneurship Public Policy, can be reached by mail at the RAND Corporation, 1776 Main Street, P.O. Box 2138, Santa Monica, CA 90407-2138; by phone at 310-393-0411, ext. 7452; by Fax at 310-451-6979; or by e-mail at Susan_Gates@rand.org. Information on the Kauffman-RAND Institute for Entrepreneurship Public Policy is available at www.rand.org/icj/centers/small_business/.

Correspondence regarding this report should be sent to the project leader, Elaine Reardon, at Elaine_Reardon@rand.org.

Contents

Tables

Summary

In 2000, the Small Business Reauthorization Act (Public Law 106-554, Section 811) authorized contracting officers to restrict competition for federal contracts on a discretionary basis in certain industries to women-owned small businesses (WOSBs). These industries are determined by the Small Business Administration (SBA) to be characterized by underrepresentation or substantial underrepresentation of WOSBs in federal prime contracts. Through a series of legal decisions, especially decisions regarding minority-owned firms, underrepresentation in government contracting has come to mean that the share of contracts awarded to a particular type of firm is small relative to the prevalence of such firms in the pool of firms that are "ready, willing, and able" to perform government contracts.

This measure of underrepresentation is typically referred to as a disparity ratio. A disparity ratio of 1.0 suggests that firms of a particular type are awarded contracts in the same proportion as their representation in the industry—that is, there is no disparity. A disparity ratio of less than 1.0 suggests that the firms are underrepresented in federal contracting, and a ratio greater than 1.0 suggests that they are overrepresented.

Measuring Disparity Ratios in Federal Contracting

The SBA asked RAND to compute disparity ratios for WOSBs based on both the dollar value and the number of contracts awarded to WOSBs. The SBA also requested that RAND define the population of firms that are ready, willing, and able to perform federal contracts in two ways: (1) as the population of all firms in the economy and (2) as the population of firms that have registered as potential bidders for federal contracts. Thus, in this report, we present disparity ratios computed in four ways: ratios based on number of contracts and on contract dollars in which the population of ready, willing, and able firms is essentially all firms, and ratios based on number of contracts and contract dollars in which the population of ready, willing, and able firms is all firms that have registered as potential bidders for federal contracts. We also explored whether there was a subset of smaller contract sizes (such as contracts under $100,000) for which it might make more sense to examine small-business contracting, but we did not find evidence of such a subset.

In this study, we compute disparity ratios by industry, defined according to the North American Industry Classification System (NAICS) at the 2-, 3-, and 4-digit levels (corresponding to increasingly disaggregated industry classifications). Following SBA guidelines, we classify WOSBs as underrepresented in industries in which the disparity ratio is between 0.5 and 0.8, and substantially underrepresented in industries in which the disparity ratio is between 0 and 0.5.

Data

We used three datasets to compute the four types of disparity ratios. The Federal Procurement Data System (FPDS) contains data on federal prime contracts over a certain size. These data can be used to compute the value of federal contracts awarded to WOSBs and all other firms. We use FPDS data from three fiscal years (FYs): FY02, FY03, and FY05. The Central Contractor Registry (CCR) lists the firms that have registered with the federal government in anticipation of bidding on federal contracts. With these data, we computed the number of ready, willing, and able WOSBs and the number of all ready, willing, and able businesses. Because the CCR data are not archived, we used the October 2006 file to compare with the most recent available contracting data in the FY05 FPDS. Finally, we constructed measures of the total number of employer businesses and women-owned employer businesses in the population, using the 2002 Survey of Business Owners (SBO), part of the 2002 Economic Census.

We did not make any adjustments to the official NAICS industry groupings; thus, dissimilar industries sometimes fall into the same code. (For example, NAICS code 6115 includes cosmetology schools as well as flight-training schools.) Finally, only industries with samples large enough to calculate significant differences across groups were analyzed.

Key Findings

We found that the measurement of whether WOSBs are underrepresented in federal contracting is sensitive to whether contract awards are measured in dollars or in number of awards and to whether the population of ready, willing, and able firms comprises essentially all employer firms or just those firms that have registered as potential bidders on federal contracts. Depending on the measure used, underrepresentation of WOSBs in government contracting occurs either in no industries or in up to 87 percent of industries. The variation is especially large in the measures that use contract dollars rather than number of contracts. This report does not advocate a particular measure. Rather, it highlights industries where disparities occur and discusses how the identification of these industries varies depending on the methodology used and on data limitations.

Acknowledgments

We wish to thank Eric Benderson and Robert Taylor of the SBA for their assistance on this project, particularly in obtaining the necessary data. We also thank RAND colleague Sue Polich for her programming assistance; Claude Setodji of RAND for his assistance with the power calculations; and David Loughran, also of RAND, for his thoughtful review. Finally, we wish to thank Constance Citro of the National Academies and two anonymous reviewers for their helpful comments. Errors in this document are solely the authors' responsibility.

Abbreviations

CCR	Central Contractor Registry
CIA	Central Intelligence Agency
FAA	Federal Aviation Administration
FDIC	Federal Deposit Insurance Corporation
FPDS	Federal Procurement Data System
FY	fiscal year
GAO	Government Accountability Office
NAICS	North American Industry Classification System
NRC	National Research Council
NSA	National Security Agency
RFP	request for proposal
SBA	Small Business Administration
SBO	Survey of Business Owners
TVA	Tennessee Valley Authority
WOB	women-owned business
WOSB	women-owned small business

CHAPTER ONE

Introduction

For more than half a century, the federal government has been concerned with the extent to which small businesses have received their "fair share" of government procurement dollars. This concern has taken a number of legislative forms, from the establishment of the Small Business Administration (SBA) in 1953 to the Business Opportunity Development Act of 1988 (Public Law 100-656, Section 502), which established a goal of at least 20 percent of overall direct federal procurement contract dollars to be awarded to small businesses. This goal was raised to 23 percent in 1997 as part of the Small Business Reauthorization Act of 1997 (Section 603). The Federal Acquisition Streamlining Act of 1994 (Public Law 103-355) set statutory goals for procurement from women-owned small businesses (WOSBs) amounting to 5 percent of prime and subcontract contract dollars for each category.

While the share of contract awards going to WOSBs has risen over time, the government has never reached its 5 percent target. Only 3.3 percent of prime contracts were awarded to WOSBs in fiscal year (FY) 2005, the most recent year for which data are available (Federal Procurement Data System, 2005). In 2000, the Small Business Reauthorization Act (Public Law 106-554, Section 811) authorized contracting officers to restrict competition for federal contracts in certain industries to WOSBs. These industries are determined by the SBA as those characterized by underrepresentation or substantial underrepresentation of WOSBs in federal procurement.

This kind of industry determination has come to be known as a disparity study. It has its origin in litigation surrounding government preferences regarding minority-owned businesses. A historical overview of the many programs Congress has enacted to assist women- and minority-owned firms, along with the history of litigation accompanying those programmatic efforts, is given in a 2005 National Research Council (NRC) report on measuring disparity. The key legal decision that prompted the undertaking of disparity studies resulted from a 1989 Supreme Court case, *City of Richmond v. J. A. Croson Co.*, in which the Court determined that state and local race-based preference programs needed to meet its "strict scrutiny standard." The set-aside programs must serve a "compelling interest" and be "narrowly tailored." States and local governments argued that such programs were needed to show that "ready, willing, and able" minority-owned firms were being underutilized. The Supreme Court then extended this level of scrutiny to federal race-based programs in a 1995 decision, *Adarand Constructors v. Pena*. Although there have been few cases concerning women-owned businesses per se, it appears that Congress assumes that a similar standard would hold—hence its stipulation that before the SBA can restrict bidding to WOSBs, it must first show that there are disparities that adversely affect them.

The SBA produced a draft industry analysis in 2002 and asked the NRC to review the report before final publication. The NRC review concluded that the SBA should reanalyze federal contracting data, using more current data, different industry classifications, and consistent utilization measures to provide more complete documentation of data and methods (National Research Council, 2005). In response, the SBA issued a request for proposal (RFP) in 2005 asking for assistance in determining the industries in which WOSBs are underrepresented in federal procurement. RAND was awarded the contract to provide that assistance.

This report presents estimates of underrepresentation of WOSBs in federal contracting, using a number of different measures. The primary finding is that estimates of underrepresentation vary widely when different measures, so-called disparity ratios, are employed. Chapter Two discusses the definition and measurement of disparity ratios. Chapter Three describes the data used in the analysis. Chapter Four presents the results of our analysis; and Chapter Five provides a brief conclusion.

CHAPTER TWO

Disparity Ratios

A disparity ratio measures the degree to which firms of a given type (e.g., women-owned) are represented in federal contracting in proportion to their prevalence in the economy at large. Simply examining the percentage of contracts going to WOSBs is widely acknowledged to be an inadequate measure of disparity: If there are no WOSBs in a particular industry, the fact that no contracts are awarded to WOSBs is indicative not of discrimination but rather of unavailability. This chapter describes how we compute four different measures of the disparity ratio.

Adopting the notation of the NRC report, disparity (D) is measured as the ratio of utilization (U) to availability (A):

$$D = U/A,$$

where $U = C_W/C_T$ and $A = W/T$, with utilization measured as the ratio of the number of contracts awarded to WOSBs (C_W) to the number of contracts awarded overall (C_T), and availability is measured as the ratio of the number of WOSBs (W) to the total number of firms (T). Utilization can also be measured as the ratio of contract dollars awarded to WOSBs relative to total contract dollars awarded. Availability is then measured as gross receipts for WOSBs relative to gross receipts for all firms. A simple, if somewhat contrived, example shows the difference between the measures. If the federal government awards 10,001 contracts, and 10,000 of those go to small businesses but the remaining contract goes to one large firm and accounts for 90 percent of the total contract dollars awarded, a disparity measure based on number of contracts would be high and one based on dollars awarded would be low. (Which measure is most appropriate depends on the policy being pursued.)

If the disparity ratio is equal to 1.0, WOSBs are awarded contracts in the same proportion as their representation in the industry—i.e., there is no disparity. If the ratio is less than 1.0, WOSBs are underrepresented as government contractors relative to their share of total business. If the ratio is greater than 1.0, WOSBs are overrepresented relative to their share of total business.

Following the example of the SBA, we classify WOSBs as underrepresented in industries in which the disparity ratio is between 0.5 and 0.8. We classify WOSBs as substantially underrepresented in industries in which the disparity ratio is less than 0.5. As the NRC review concludes, there is no hard and fast rule for where to draw those lines, and the SBA definitions are reasonable.

Utilization and Availability

To construct a disparity ratio, we must define each of its components of utilization and availability. First, however, we must define a WOSB. The SBA definition of a small business, for federal contracting purposes, varies by industry. In manufacturing, mining, and wholesale trade, the definition is based on the number of employees. Firms with fewer than 500 employees are considered small in manufacturing, and firms with fewer than 100 employees are considered small in wholesale trade. Annual revenue is used to define small firms in many other industries, such as construction (less than \$28.5 million), retail trade (less than \$6 million) and service firms (less than \$6 million). The subset of small businesses that are women-owned comprises those of which at least 51 percent is owned by women. One can imagine scenarios in which the number of women-owned or small firms is overstated because firms wish to present themselves that way in order to receive preferential treatment in SBA programs. One can also imagine that characteristics of firms can change over time without any intent to "game the system," through firm contraction and expansion, ownership changes, mergers, and the like. This report does not address these errors of classification.

We vary our measures of utilization and availability to create four basic kinds of ratio. First, we derive disparity ratios based on the dollar value of awarded contracts. These are shown as 1 and 3 in Table 2.1. Second, we use number of contracts awarded to measure utilization. These are shown as 2 and 4 in the table.

A key decision in the derivation of disparity ratios is determining how to estimate availability. The first (and broader) method estimates the share of WOSBs in the economy. The second estimates the share of WOSBs among the set of ready, willing, and able firms. Which method is appropriate depends on the mechanisms thought to be at work. Disparity ratios do not measure discrimination itself, they measure the difference between men and women in some dimension, in this case, in winning federal government contracts. The difference could be due to a number of reasons, only some of which are discriminatory. For example, women might be more interested than men in industries where the federal government does not spend a lot of money, or they may be less interested in working with the government. These factors suggest that the second method—focusing on ready, willing, and able firms—might be the correct one to use. Discrimination in the awarding of contracts, however, might result from

Table 2.1
Four Ways to Measure Disparity

	Utilization	
Availability	Contract Dollars	Number of Contracts
Survey of Business Owners (SBO) employer firms	1	2
Central Contractor Registry (CCR) registrants	3	4

women business owners being less likely to bid on contracts. This would not be detected if the pool of available firms consists only of firms that have demonstrated their interest by bidding on contracts. Again, the disparity ratio can only measure the difference; it cannot explain it.

The SBA requested that RAND define the population of firms that are ready, willing, and able to perform federal contracts in two ways. The first is the population of all firms in the economy (disparity ratios 1 and 2 in Table 2.1). The second is the population of firms that have registered as potential bidders for federal contracts (ratios 3 and 4 in the table). Thus, in this report, we compute disparity ratios four ways: by contract-dollars and number-of-contracts ratios in which the population of ready, willing, and able firms is essentially all firms, and by contract-dollars and number-of-contracts ratios in which the population of such firms is all firms that have registered as potential bidders for federal contracts.

Disaggregating Disparity Ratios by Industry

Disparity ratios are calculated by industry, because conditions vary by industry. For example, WOSBs (and small businesses generally) are more prevalent in the service sector than in heavy manufacturing, where the costs of entry are higher due to the sheer scale of production (Lowry, 2006). The SBA draft report presented its findings using 2-digit North American Industry Classification System (NAICS) industry codes. The NRC review of that draft concluded that, where possible, results should also be presented using 3- and 4-digit industry codes. By "where possible," they meant that there should be enough firms in the code to analyze statistically and be reasonably sure that random chance did not explain the result, and also that the firms grouped in the code performed fairly similar activities. We report our results by 2-digit industries and by 3- and 4-digit industries when the data allow. We have made no adjustments to industry groupings, but we note that dissimilar businesses are more likely to be grouped together at higher levels of aggregation. Even at the 4-digit level, some dissimilar firms are grouped together (e.g., cosmetology schools and flight-instruction schools). Because any determination we might make would be ad hoc, we chose not to make adjustments to the official codes. However, we did test for adequate sample size.

CHAPTER THREE

Data Sources

A number of datasets must be used to construct disparity ratios for federal contracting. The Federal Procurement Data System (FPDS) contains data on federal contract actions. The Central Contractor Registry (CCR) lists the firms that have registered with the federal government in anticipation of bidding on contracts. The 2002 Survey of Business Owners (SBO), part of the 2002 Economic Census, publishes aggregate data on the universe of businesses in the United States. In this chapter, we discuss each dataset in turn, outlining the content and methodology underlying each and the decisions we made in creating analysis files.

The Federal Procurement Data System

The FPDS contains individual contract actions on prime contracts above a certain size for federal procurement. Most federal agencies use this system.[1] In FY05, these contracts amounted to over $300 billion in procurement spending. Historically, the FPDS collected information on contracts over $25,000. In FY04, a new data system was launched that, in addition to changing the user interface, began to collect data on contracts over $2,500. The strength of the FPDS is that it is our best source for information on federal contracts, and it contains the data used to determine whether federal procurement has met the goals set for it by Congress. Its limitations for small-business analysis are well known: It contains data only on prime contracts, not subcontracts; it does not include some very small contracts (under $25,000 or $2,500, depending on the year); and it has only begun to collect purchase-card data.

The FPDS records most contract actions for federal prime contracts above a certain dollar amount in a fiscal year. The action-level data can be rolled up into contracts to count the number of contracts and their dollar amount. Until FY04, transactions below $25,000 were reported on a different form and only in the aggregate, meaning those data cannot be used for disparity studies. Nevertheless, the majority of dollars awarded are recorded in the FPDS. When agencies began to report on contracts above $2,500 in the FPDS, beginning in FY04,

[1] Those that do not include Congress, the Government Accountability Office (GAO), the Central Intelligence Agency (CIA), the National Security Agency (NSA), the courts, the Federal Aviation Administration (FAA), the Tennessee Valley Authority (TVA), and the Federal Deposit Insurance Corporation (FDIC).

small-business representation was much improved, compared with earlier years.[2] There is still some procurement from small firms that is not recorded in the FPDS. For example, agencies can use purchase cards for small purchases. Only some agencies report these data in the most recent version of the FPDS (earlier versions did not collect purchase-card data), and the data are not combined in the contract file. Finally, the FPDS includes data on only prime contracts, not subcontracts, which tend to be smaller and to rely relatively more on small businesses. This is especially regrettable in industries such as manufacturing, where subsectors such as parts manufacturing exhibit much higher small-business participation than does large-scale manufacturing (e.g., aircraft engines rather than entire aircraft). Despite these caveats, the FPDS remains our best source for analyzing federal contracting with small firms, and indeed, these are the data used to report on the extent to which the federal government is meeting congressional goals for targeted procurement.

We used three files for our analysis: those for FY02, FY03, and FY05. We used the FY02 and FY03 data to create WOSB utilization for comparison with availability measures constructed using the 2002 SBO. We constructed the ratios separately by year to determine whether the FY02 and FY03 files could be safely combined across years; the results were not similar in all industries, so we did not combine the years.

Industries are coded in the FPDS using 6-digit NAICS codes, which classify industries at the 2-digit sector level, 3-digit subsector levels, and 4-digit industry groups, as well as into 5- and 6-digit industries. The NAICS replaced the older (1987) Standard Industrial Classification System. In 2002, the NAICS codes were substantially revised in the construction and wholesale trade sectors, and minor changes were made to retail trade and the information sector. The changes did not affect the 2-digit categorizations, however. Thus, although the FY02 file uses the 1997 version of NAICS codes, it can be used in conjunction with the 2-digit-level 2002 NAICS codes used in the SBO to create disparity ratios.

We used the most recent FPDS file, FY05, to compare with the CCR data. The version we used contains records as of October 2006; additional records are sometimes added to the FPDS file later, as contract situations resolve themselves. We do not anticipate that this would change our results in any substantive way.

We rolled up the data from individual actions into contracts based on the contract numbers in the file, excluding observations with invalid or missing NAICS codes. In some cases, individual actions refer to multiyear contracts or are revisions to earlier contracts. This can lead to errors in summing to the contract level, such as negative dollar amounts or very large contract values. However, our comparisons from FY02 through FY05 also indicate that very large contracts and larger negative values are awarded each year, suggesting that they are not outliers. The NRC report was concerned with the effect extreme values might have on the disparity ratios. To examine the sensitivity of the disparity ratios to such values, we trimmed the top and bottom 0.5 percent of contract awards after rolling up the data to the contract level. We show these results, but without a compelling reason to delete these contracts, we are inclined to put more weight on the full-sample results.

---

[2] The Army began reporting transactions above $2,500 in FY03, and the Marine Corps began to do so in FY04, but most other services and agencies did not report such transactions until FY05.

We made some adjustments to the FPDS to account for miscoding of business size. A 2004 report by Eagle Eye Publishers noted considerable miscoding of small-business size in the FPDS, particularly cases of large firms being coded as small (Eagle Eye Publishers, Inc., 2004). For our analyses, we linked the FPDS data to 2004 Dun and Bradstreet data that linked parent companies and local establishments and used the Dun and Bradstreet assessment of whether a firm was small. However, the Dun and Bradstreet DUNS file[3] is also prone to error, and it is not clear which definition of small is more accurate. Therefore, we show results with and without the DUNS.[4] It is also possible to link the FY05 FPDS and CCR data, and we experimented with using the CCR definitions of women-owned and small business in our analysis file.

There are other data coding errors in the FPDS data that we were unable to correct, such as contract awards that contain purchases of both goods and services that are characterized with a single NAICS code. Dixon et al. (2005) found that nearly 50 percent of a sample of FY02 Air Force contracts were coded inaccurately and that services were less likely than goods to be coded as the contract's NAICS code. These types of coding errors will tend to bias disparity ratios in service industries downward if WOSBs are more likely to provide services than goods.

Tables 3.1 through 3.6 provide summary statistics for the FY02 FPDS and FY05 FPDS, separately by contracts to WOSBs, other small firms, and large firms. The tables show that WOSBs have fewer contracts and that the contracts they have tend to be smaller than those of other firms on average. The wide variation in contract values is evident in the magnitude of the difference between mean and median contract values for all three groups, all of which have a high fraction of contracts under $100,000 as well. Industry distributions of contracts are far more similar across groups than they are in the wider economy, where women are far less concentrated in manufacturing and are more prevalent in services (see Table 3.10, below). This is not surprising given the nature of government procurement.

Table 3.1
Summary Contract Statistics for FY02 FPDS

	Women-Owned Small Firms	Men-Owned Small Firms	Large Firms
Number of firms	13,984	89,307	66,852
Mean value	$337,100	$360,270	$1,937,185
Median value	$50,000	$54,000	$86,000
Minimum	–$7,640,000	–$49,700,000	–$317,000,000
Maximum	$118,000,000	$215,000,000	$1,970,000,000
Percentage under $100,000	69.5	68.6	55.2

NOTE: These summary statistics were calculated for the FY02 FPDS analysis file after all sample adjustments and deletions were made.

[3] A DUNS number is a unique nine-digit sequence for identifying and keeping track of businesses.

[4] In the FY02 FPDS, 4 percent of contracts coded as WOSBs are considered non-WOSBs when the Dun and Bradstreet file is also used.

Table 3.2
Industry Distribution of Contracts in FY02 FPDS

2-Digit Code	Industry	Women-Owned Small Firms (percent)	Men-Owned Small Firms (percent)	Large Firms (percent)
11	Forestry, fishing	1.0	1.7	0.2
21	Mining	0.2	0.2	0.2
22	Utilities	0.3	0.3	2.6
23	Construction	15.9	15.2	7.2
31–33	Manufacturing	27.2	35.1	35.2
42	Wholesale trade	6.8	5.6	4.2
44–45	Retail trade	2.2	1.8	1.2
48–49	Transportation and warehousing	1.3	1.8	2.2
51	Information	2.4	2.3	3.8
52	Finance and insurance	0.1	0.1	0.2
53	Real estate	1.6	4.3	3.4
54	Prof., sci., and tech. services	20.5	19.6	21.7
55	Management of companies	0.0	0.0	0.0
56	Admin. and waste management services	11.1	6.1	5.8
61	Educational services	1.3	0.7	2.3
62	Health care and social assistance	4.9	2.8	5.9
71	Arts and recreation	0.7	0.2	0.2
72	Accom. and food services	0.9	0.6	0.9
81	Other services (except public administration)	1.6	1.8	3.0
99	Other	0.0	0.0	0.1
Total		100.0	100.0	100.0
N		13,984	89,307	66,852

NOTE: These summary statistics were calculated for the FY02 FPDS analysis file after all sample adjustments and deletions were made.

Table 3.3
Industry Distribution of Contract Dollars in FY02 FPDS

2-Digit Code	Industry	Women-Owned Small Firms (percent)	Men-Owned Small Firms (percent)	Large Firms (percent)
11	Forestry, fishing	0.2	0.5	0.0
21	Mining	0.1	0.4	0.1
22	Utilities	0.3	0.2	0.9
23	Construction	13.6	14.7	5.8
31–33	Manufacturing	17.5	26.1	34.4
42	Wholesale trade	3.0	3.1	3.0
44–45	Retail trade	2.5	2.5	1.2
48–49	Transportation and warehousing	0.6	2.6	1.9
51	Information	5.5	3.5	2.7
52	Finance and insurance	0.0	0.0	0.9
53	Real estate	3.2	4.2	1.2
54	Prof., sci., and tech. services	35.5	31.5	33.8
55	Management of companies	0.0	0.0	0.0
56	Admin. and waste management services	13.3	8.2	11.4
61	Educational services	0.0	0.4	0.7
62	Health care and social assistance	1.9	0.8	0.7
71	Arts and recreation	0.2	0.1	0.1
72	Accom. and food services	1.5	0.4	0.3
81	Other services (except public administration)	0.7	0.8	0.8
99	Other	0.1	0.0	0.0
Total		100.0	100.0	100.0
N		13,984	89,307	66,852

NOTE: These summary statistics were calculated for the FY02 FPDS analysis file after all sample adjustments and deletions were made.

Table 3.4
Summary Contract Statistics for FY05 FPDS

	Women-Owned Small Firms	Men-Owned Small Firms	Large Firms
Number	87,828	339,187	219,445
Mean value	$69,422	$110,811	$719,308
Median value	$4,607	$6,840	$8,085
Minimum	–$1,319,870	–$13,500,000	-$93,500,000
Maximum	$141,000,000	$490,000,000	$5,250,000,000
Percentage under $100,000	93.7	91.8	87.9

NOTE: These summary statistics were calculated for the FY05 FPDS analysis file after all sample adjustments and deletions were made.

Table 3.5
Industry Distribution of Contracts in FY05 FPDS

2-Digit Code	Industry	Women-Owned Small Firms (percent)	Men-Owned Small Firms (percent)	Large Firms (percent)
11	Forestry, fishing	0.6	0.8	0.5
21	Mining	0.1	0.2	0.2
22	Utilities	0.2	0.4	1.5
23	Construction	4.4	5.5	4.0
31	Manufacturing	1.5	1.9	1.9
32	Manufacturing	9.5	5.6	5.0
33	Manufacturing	48.0	47.4	34.6
42	Wholesale trade	8.3	9.2	8.7
44	Retail trade	1.9	2.1	2.3
45	Retail trade	1.0	1.0	1.0
48	Transportation and warehousing	0.7	1.1	1.6
49	Transportation and warehousing	0.3	0.2	0.4
51	Information	1.0	1.9	3.6
52	Finance and insurance	0.1	0.1	0.4
53	Real estate	1.3	2.0	3.0
54	Prof., sci., and tech. services	9.0	9.8	11.7
55	Management of companies	0.0	0.0	0.0
56	Admin. and waste management services	5.5	4.0	4.8
61	Educational services	1.5	1.3	2.7
62	Health care and social assistance	1.5	1.0	3.1
71	Arts and recreation	0.6	0.3	0.4
72	Accom. and food services	1.0	1.3	2.5
81	Other services (except public administration)	1.8	2.7	4.6
92	Public administration	0.3	0.4	1.5
99	Other	0.0	0.0	0.0
Total		100.0	100.0	100.0
N		87,828	339,187	219,445

NOTE: These summary statistics were calculated for the FY05 FPDS analysis file after all sample adjustments and deletions were made.

Table 3.6
Industry Distribution of Contract Dollars in FY05 FPDS

2-Digit Code	Industry	Women-Owned Small Firms (percent)	Men-Owned Small Firms (percent)	Large Firms (percent)
11	Forestry, fishing	0.4	0.3	0.1
21	Mining	0.2	0.1	0.0
22	Utilities	0.3	0.5	0.6
23	Construction	16.9	16.6	6.0
31	Manufacturing	1.5	3.3	0.9
32	Manufacturing	0.8	2.4	0.6
33	Manufacturing	16.5	22.9	37.8
42	Wholesale trade	5.6	2.2	0.7
44	Retail trade	0.7	0.8	0.2
45	Retail trade	0.2	0.2	0.1
48	Transportation and warehousing	1.1	1.4	1.3
49	Transportation and warehousing	0.2	0.2	0.2
51	Information	1.4	2.1	1.1
52	Finance and insurance	0.3	0.1	0.1
53	Real estate	3.2	1.1	0.5
54	Prof., sci., and tech. services	33.0	31.5	31.2
55	Management of companies	0.0	0.0	0.0
56	Admin. and waste management services	12.3	9.5	13.7
61	Educational services	1.1	1.2	1.4
62	Health care and social assistance	2.1	1.2	0.9
71	Arts and recreation	0.2	0.1	0.0
72	Accom. and food services	1.2	0.6	0.3
81	Other services (except public administration)	0.8	0.9	1.0
92	Public administration	0.1	0.8	1.4
99	Other	0.0	0.0	0.1
Total		100.0	100.0	100.0
N		87,828	339,187	219,445

NOTE: These summary statistics were calculated for the FY05 FPDS analysis file after all sample adjustments and deletions were made.

Central Contractor Registry

A common way of defining a group of firms as ready, willing, and able to compete for government contracts is to use bidder lists, under the assumption that these firms will at least be ready and willing. The CCR is a database of vendors that have federal government contracts or would like to bid on contracts. The vendor is asked to report its type of business, relevant NAICS codes, DUNS number, taxpayer identification number, address, start date, annual employment, and three-year average annual revenue. The vendor can also describe itself along a number of socioeconomic dimensions, including whether it is women-owned. The SBA then uses the self-reported employment and revenue figures to determine whether the firm is small, based on the official industry size standards.[5] Vendors must renew their information once a year, and expired records are purged after 18 months.

We deleted firms from the sample if they reported annual revenue of less than $1,000 (the cut-off the Census Bureau uses in fielding the SBO) or more than $380 billion (approximately the size of Exxon), or if they reported having more than 1.9 million employees (approximately the size of Wal-Mart).[6] For firms that maintained entries for multiple establishments, we kept only one entry, because the records were identical (i.e., employment, revenue, start date) except for the location. We also deleted duplicate records.[7] Finally, we deleted vendors that competed only for grants.

To evaluate whether the firms on this list are able, we examined employment and revenue patterns to determine whether any firms listed appeared unable to successfully compete for contracts. We did not discover an obvious way to make this determination. On average, small firms are younger, have fewer employees, have lower revenue, and win smaller contracts. The degree of overlap is high, however, with some "small" firms reporting 337,000 employees and some "large" firms reporting one employee. Wide variation is also present in firm start dates, with 1 percent of firms reporting start dates before 1866, 10 percent before 1956, and 50 percent by 1993. Tables 3.7, 3.8, and 3.9 report summary statistics from the CCR. Table 3.7 shows that WOSBs tend to be smaller in terms of both employment and revenue. Table 3.8 shows the distribution of firms by industry and ownership. Table 3.9 shows the distribution of gross revenue of firms by industry and ownership.

Table 3.7
Summary Firm Statistics from the CCR

	Women-Owned Small Firms	Men-Owned Small Firms	Large Firms
N	55,896	221,048	79,945
Employment			
Mean value	18	47	7,840
Median value	4	7	100
Minimum	1	1	1
Maximum	150,200	337,000	1,325,023
Revenue			
Mean value, $	3,715,272	12,300,000	1,060,000,000
Median value, $	300,000	790,000	12,300,000
Minimum, $	1,000	1,000	1,000
Maximum, $	35,000,000,000	225,000,000,000	370,000,000,000

NOTE: These summary statistics were calculated for the CCR analysis file after all sample adjustments and deletions were made.

[5] We counted a firm as small if it was coded as a Small Business, SBA Certified Small Disadvantaged Business, SBA certified 8(a) Program Participant, or Emerging Small Business.

[6] Exxon and Wal-Mart are the largest U.S. firms, measured in revenues and employment, respectively.

[7] In most cases, firms with duplicate records appeared to be testing the user interface.

Table 3.8
Industry Distribution of Firms in the CCR

2-Digit Code	Industry	Women-Owned Small Firms (percent)	Men-Owned Small Firms (percent)	Large Firms (percent)
11	Forestry, fishing	0.8	1.6	1.1
21	Mining	0.1	0.3	0.2
22	Utilities	0.1	0.3	2.1
23	Construction	7.6	10.6	5.2
31	Manufacturing	1.0	1.2	1.2
32	Manufacturing	1.9	2.6	1.7
33	Manufacturing	8.4	13.0	8.6
42	Wholesale trade	5.6	6.3	4.6
44	Retail trade	2.7	3.1	6.4
45	Retail trade	2.3	1.8	3.0
48	Transportation and warehousing	2.4	2.7	2.3
49	Transportation and warehousing	0.7	0.7	0.5
51	Information	1.6	2.4	2.3
52	Finance and insurance	0.3	0.4	1.2
53	Real estate	2.5	4.4	3.9
54	Prof., sci., and tech. services	21.2	18.9	11.0
55	Management of companies	0.0	0.0	0.2
56	Admin. and waste management services	15.5	10.0	6.2
61	Educational services	7.1	3.7	6.0
62	Health care and social assistance	4.8	4.3	8.5
71	Arts and recreation	2.8	1.3	1.4
72	Accom. and food services	1.6	2.0	3.4
81	Other services (except public administration)	6.7	7.3	8.8
92	Public administration	2.4	1.5	10.5
Total		100.0	100.0	100.0
N		55,896	221,048	79,945

NOTE: These summary statistics were calculated for the CCR analysis file after all sample adjustments and deletions were made.

Survey of Business Owners

The SBO is a part of the Economic Census, which collects data about business owners for all firms (not establishments) with $1,000 or more in gross receipts. Most businesses are surveyed; sole-proprietorships data are obtained from Schedule C income tax records. Economic Census data include owners' gender, race, and ethnicity; owners' education; type of business; ownership structure; employment; payroll; gross receipts; and startup capital. The response rate is 81 percent; missing data are imputed from respondents reporting similar characteristics. The SBO is public-use data and contains only aggregate data for a subset of characteristics. (Access to the confidential individual-firm-level data must be coordinated with the Census Bureau and can

Table 3.9
Industry Distribution of Revenue in the CCR

2-Digit Code	Industry	Women-Owned Small Firms (percent)	Men-Owned Small Firms (percent)	Large Firms (percent)
11	Forestry, fishing	0.1	0.1	0.1
21	Mining	0.1	0.5	0.1
22	Utilities	0.1	2.2	0.7
23	Construction	3.8	2.8	1.9
31	Manufacturing	10.0	5.5	1.1
32	Manufacturing	2.2	9.1	3.1
33	Manufacturing	16.1	25.7	16.3
42	Wholesale trade	12.9	12.1	5.6
44	Retail trade	4.4	3.9	17.1
45	Retail trade	3.2	5.6	5.9
48	Transportation and warehousing	1.1	6.6	1.0
49	Transportation and warehousing	0.3	0.6	9.3
51	Information	2.7	3.0	2.5
52	Finance and insurance	0.1	0.2	1.9
53	Real estate	0.8	1.2	2.0
54	Prof., sci., and tech. services	7.7	6.3	15.5
55	Management of companies	0.0	0.0	0.7
56	Admin. and waste management services	22.7	4.3	4.1
61	Educational services	1.4	2.9	1.1
62	Health care and social assistance	1.5	1.1	1.0
71	Arts and recreation	0.2	0.1	0.5
72	Accom. and food services	0.4	0.4	2.0
81	Other services (except public administration)	6.6	5.3	4.1
92	Public administration	1.5	0.6	2.5
Total		100.0	100.0	100.0
N		55,896	221,048	79,945

NOTE: These summary statistics were calculated for the CCR analysis file after all sample adjustments and deletions were made.

take a considerable amount of time to arrange.) A firm is considered women-owned if 51 percent or more of it is owned by women.[8] Industries are coded using the 2002 NAICS codes.

The following industries are excluded from the SBO: agricultural production, domestically scheduled airlines, railroads, U.S. Postal Service, mutual funds (except real estate investment trusts), religious grant operations, private households and religious organizations, public administration, and government. These industries were also excluded from the FY02 and FY03 FPDS in our analysis because we could not construct a measure of availability. The published SBO also groups certain 2-digit industries, so we grouped the FPDS similarly.[9]

[8] The SBO also publishes data on firms that are owned equally by men and women. Sixty-four percent of employer firms are majority-owned by men, 17 percent are owned by women, 13 percent are owned equally, and the rest are publicly held.

[9] Manufacturing spans codes 31–33, but data are published for all three together. The same is true in retail (codes 44 and 45) and transportation and warehousing (codes 48 and 49).

We explored different ways of narrowing the comparison group to firms that are ready, willing, and able but concluded that there was no good way of doing this beyond limiting the sample to firms with paid employees.[10] There are two reasons for this. First, there is substantial overlap among small and large firms in the distribution of contract size, revenue, and employment. When we linked FPDS and CCR data to identify small firms that have been successful in winning contracts, we could not find a natural break point in contract size beyond which small businesses generally could not compete (e.g., above $100,000 or $200,000). We also found substantial overlap in small and large firms' distributions of revenue and employment. Both large and small firms in the linked file reported from one to more than 337,000 employees. That is our second reason for limiting the sample to employer firms: In the CCR, all but three firms with more than $1,000 in annual revenue report at least one employee. Sizable error in start dates also prevented us from identifying young firms to pull out of the ready, willing, and able category.

The SBO data are published at a highly aggregated level, which makes it difficult to adjust the sample. The Census Bureau publishes some information about women-owned firms by employment size (e.g., no employees, one to four employees, etc.) and revenue size. Unfortunately, this level of detail does not correspond well with SBA definitions of small firms by industry. For example, in industries where the SBA cutoff is 100 or 500 employees, we can determine the number of WOSBs because they coincide with the SBO size categories. In the service sector, where small-business activity is higher, the SBA cutoff is usually around receipts of $6.5 million. The SBO, however, reports only the number of women-owned businesses (WOBs) with more than $1 million in receipts. We restrict our use of SBO data to women-owned firms with paid employees, as a way of taking the ready, willing, and able issue into consideration and because in the CCR, virtually all firms report at least one employee. According to the 2002 SBO, 14 percent of women-owned firms have employees, and that subset earns 85 percent of the revenue generated by all women-owned businesses.

More important perhaps than whether we could make additional adjustments to the data regarding firms' readiness, the way the data are published and the fact that the reporting does not align to SBA categories meant that we could not identify WOSBs for all industries even at the 2-digit level. In other words, in the availability measure, we could count only the number of and revenue of WOBs, not WOSBs. This means that our disparity ratios using the SBO are biased downward, toward finding underrepresentation. The bias is considerably smaller for the ratios constructed using the number of contracts and firms than for those constructed using contract dollars and firm revenue. Most women-owned firms are also small firms, just as most men-owned firms are small firms. Even among women-owned firms with employees, only 1.8 percent had receipts over $1 million, and less than 0.1 percent had more than 500 employees. Numerically, small firms dominate the economy. For the most part, then, using WOBs instead of WOSBs in the denominator is reasonable. However, large firms generate most of the revenue in any industry, so WOBs are not an ideal proxy for WOSBs when we turn to measures using dollars rather than quantities. Table 3.10 shows the industry distribution of firms in

---

[10] One anonymous reviewer pointed out that the exclusion of non-employer firms may be less crucial for detecting small-business activity in our analysis than it might be in other analyses, because we were able to study only prime contracts.

Table 3.10
Industry Distribution in the SBO

		Percentage of Firms		Percentage of Receipts	
2-Digit Code	Industry	Women-Owned Firms	All Other Firms	Women-Owned Firms	All Other Firms
11	Forestry, fishing	0.3	0.6	0.2	0.1
21	Mining	0.2	0.4	0.3	1.2
22	Utilities	0.0	0.1	0.1	2.0
23	Construction	5.6	14.7	7.8	5.5
31–33	Manufacturing	4.4	5.9	11.4	18.6
42	Wholesale trade	4.6	6.6	25.7	21.6
44–45	Retail trade	15.9	13.0	16.4	14.1
48–49	Transportation and warehousing	2.1	3.2	2.4	1.8
51	Information	1.2	1.4	2.5	4.3
52	Finance and insurance	3.5	4.5	2.7	13.5
53	Real estate	5.4	4.7	3.0	1.5
54	Prof., sci., and tech. services	14.5	12.9	7.1	4.1
55	Management of companies	0.2	0.6	0.2	0.7
56	Admin. and waste management services	6.6	5.3	5.1	1.9
61	Educational services	1.7	1.1	0.7	0.7
62	Health care and social assistance	12.7	9.7	6.4	5.0
71	Arts and recreation	1.8	1.9	1.0	0.6
72	Accom. and food services	9.5	7.5	4.5	2.0
81	Other services (except public administration)	9.4	6.7	2.4	0.8
99	Other	0.7	0.5	0.1	0.0
Total		100.4	101.4	100.0	100.0
N		916,768	4,608,045	916,768	4,608,045

NOTE: These summary statistics were calculated using 1992 SBO data on employer firms.

the SBO separately for women-owned firms and for all other firms. The difference between looking at number of firms and looking at revenue is reflected here. For example, the wholesale trade industry comprises only 4.6 percent of all women-owned firms, but 25.7 percent of total receipts for women-owned firms are generated in this industry.

Constructing Disparity Ratios in This Study

We combined several datasets to produce a number of different disparity ratios, as noted in Table 3.11. As stated in Chapter Two, we used 0.8 and 0.5 as our indicators of underrepresentation and substantial underrepresentation, respectively. We then examined the extent to which this industry determination is sensitive to the way the ratio is measured.

Table 3.11
Data Used to Create Various Disparity Ratios

	Utilization	
Availability	**Contract Dollars**	**Number of Contracts**
SBO employer firms	FY02 FPDS, SBO	FY02 FPDS, SBO
CCR registrants	FY05 FPDS, CCR	FY05 FPDS, CCR

CHAPTER FOUR

Results

This chapter presents the results of our analyses. We attempted to gauge the sensitivity of these estimates to various alterations in scope and data. First, key results are presented for the set using data from the SBO (ratios based on number of contracts and then contract dollars), then key results are given for the set using the CCR (again, ratios based on number of contracts and then contract dollars). The full set of results is given in Appendix B.

Broad Definition of Ready, Willing, and Able

We first present ratios based on number of contracts where the population of ready, willing, and able firms is defined as those with paid employees operating in the United States. A finding that WOSBs are underrepresented in federal procurement contracting when we use ratios defined this way could result from a number of processes, including discrimination in federal contracting, lack of access to capital markets, and lack of knowledge about or disinterest in government contracting opportunities.

Table 4.1 reports disparity ratios by 2-digit industry code and by whether extreme values are trimmed from the sample. Disparity ratios based on whether we define small business according to the FPDS alone or whether the small-business designator in the FPDS is confirmed by the Dun and Bradstreet data are also given.[1] For ease of use, ratios that indicate substantial underrepresentation of WOSBs (between 0.0 and 0.5) are highlighted in dark gray, and those that indicate underrepresentation (between 0.5 and 0.8) are highlighted in light gray.

We find that with one exception, the conclusion that WOSBs are underrepresented in some industries is not dependent on the possible error in the definition of small firms in the FPDS. In manufacturing, the result does change a small amount, enough to move it in the trimmed sample from underrepresentation to substantial underrepresentation. However, given that we know these measures are biased downward (because we can isolate only WOBs in the SBO and not WOSBs), we are inclined to interpret this result as underrepresentation (not substantial underrepresentation).

[1] We experimented with combining FY02 and FY03 FPDS data to increase sample size. The results, given in Appendix B, show that the findings change substantively in some industries when the data are combined.

Table 4.1
Disparity Ratios Using Number of Contracts and a Broad Definition of Availability

2-Digit Code	Industry	All Contracts: FPDS	All Contracts: FPDS and DUNS	Trimmed Sample: FPDS	Trimmed Sample: FPDS and DUNS
11	Forestry, fishing	0.92	0.91	0.92	0.90
21	Mining	0.85	0.82	0.86	0.83
22	Utilities	0.47	0.45	0.47	0.45
23	Construction	1.53	1.49	1.53	1.50
31–33	Manufacturing	0.50	0.48	0.51	0.49
42	Wholesale trade	0.90	0.86	0.90	0.87
44–45	Retail trade	0.58	0.55	0.58	0.56
48–49	Transportation and warehousing	0.49	0.48	0.49	0.48
51	Information	0.49	0.47	0.49	0.47
52	Finance and insurance	0.26	0.23	0.28	0.24
53	Real estate	0.19	0.18	0.19	0.18
54	Prof., sci., and tech. services	0.45	0.42	0.45	0.43
56	Admin. and waste management services	0.72	0.69	0.72	0.70
61	Educational services	0.31	0.31	0.31	0.31
62	Health care and social assistance	0.47	0.46	0.47	0.46
71	Arts and recreation	1.66	1.64	1.66	1.64
72	Accom. and food services	0.48	0.46	0.48	0.45
81	Other services (except public administration)	0.27	0.26	0.27	0.26

NOTE: The disparity ratios are ratios of utilization to availability (U/A). Utilization is measured as the number of contracts awarded to WOSBs divided by the number of contracts in that industry, using FY02 FPDS data. Availability is measured as the number of women-owned employer firms divided by the number of all employer firms in that industry, using 2002 SBO data. Ratios between 0.0 and 0.5 are highlighted in dark gray, and those between 0.5 and 0.8 are highlighted in light gray. Industries listed are those for which our power calculations indicated there were enough data to detect a small effect. For more information about the power tests, see Appendix A.

Overall, however, trimming the sample does not affect the ratios, so, as noted in the previous chapter, we put more weight on the full-sample results than on the trimmed-sample results because of the difficulty of detecting unusual or error-dominated observations. Thus, using this measure, we find that WOSBs are substantially underrepresented in utilities, manufacturing, transportation, information services, finance, real estate, professional services, education, health, accomodations, and other services. WOSBs appear to be underrepresented in retail and administrative services.

Table 4.2 reports disparity ratios based on contract dollars, using the same broad definition of ready, willing, and able. The ratios are more sensitive to trimming the sample than to the definition of a small business, as was true in Table 4.1. WOSBs are found to be underrepresented in forestry and real estate and substantially underrepresented in transportation and other services. The extent of underrepresentation is unclear in administrative services, professional services, and educational services.

Using dollars rather than number of contracts and firms leads to a different conclusion about industries in which WOSBs are underrepresented, except in transportation and other services, results for which are consistent across the various measures. Our goal at the outset was

Table 4.2
Disparity Ratios Using Contract Dollars and a Broad Definition of Availability

2-Digit Code	Industry	All Contracts FPDS	All Contracts FPDS and DUNS	Trimmed Sample FPDS	Trimmed Sample FPDS and DUNS
11	Forestry, fishing	0.73	0.72	0.75	0.74
21	Mining	0.99	0.95	0.96	0.92
22	Utilities	6.26	6.14	7.85	7.70
23	Construction	0.96	0.93	1.24	1.20
31-33	Manufacturing	0.67	0.62	1.33	1.22
42	Wholesale trade	0.65	0.57	1.07	0.94
44-45	Retail trade	1.13	1.09	2.73	2.64
48-49	Transportation and warehousing	0.17	0.18	0.42	0.41
51	Information	2.37	2.02	3.30	3.21
52	Finance and insurance	0.18	0.15	1.73	1.50
53	Real estate	0.69	0.68	0.52	0.51
54	Prof., sci., and tech. services	0.48	0.37	0.81	0.69
56	Admin. and waste management services	0.38	0.36	0.74	0.70
61	Educational services	0.71	0.51	1.06	0.76
62	Health care and social assistance	1.49	1.47	1.60	1.58
71	Arts and recreation	0.83	0.83	1.15	1.15
72	Accom. and food services	1.47	1.38	2.48	2.33
81	Other services (except public administration)	0.26	0.25	0.36	0.35

NOTE: The disparity ratios are ratios of utilization to availability (U/A). Utilization is measured as the dollars in contracts awarded to WOSBs divided by the dollars in that industry, using FY02 FPDS data. Availability is measured as the revenue of women-owned employer firms divided by the revenue of all employer firms in that industry, using 2002 SBO data. Ratios between 0.0 and 0.5 are highlighted in dark gray, and those between 0.5 and 0.8 are highlighted in light gray. Industries listed are those for which our power calculations indicated there were enough data to detect a small effect and the FDPS contained contracts. For more information about the power tests, see Appendix A.

to gauge the sensitivity of our conclusions to changes in measurement, and there is no question that the ratios are indeed sensitive.

Narrower Definition of Ready, Willing, and Able

Next we report disparity ratios found when we define the population of firms that are ready, willing, and able to perform federal contracts as those firms that are registered in the CCR. Table 4.3 presents disparity ratios based on number of contracts. In general, use of this measure shows widespread underrepresentation of WOSBs in government contracting, except in forestry and some kinds of manufacturing. The trimmed sample shows much more sensitivity to the DUNS correction than the full sample does, though we cannot provide any intuition about why that might be the case. Apart from that, the measures are fairly consistent. WOSBs are underrepresented in construction, wholesale trade, one retail trade subsector (44), real estate, health, arts, and accommodations. They are substantially underrepresented in utilities,

Table 4.3
Disparity Ratios Using Number of Contracts and a Narrow Definition of Availability

		All Contracts		Trimmed Sample	
2-Digit Code	Industry	FPDS	FPDS and DUNS	FPDS	FPDS and DUNS
11	Forestry, fishing	0.88	0.88	0.88	0.93
21	Mining	0.63	0.62	0.63	1.15
22	Utilities	0.34	0.33	0.34	0.25
23	Construction	0.79	0.78	0.79	0.65
31	Manufacturing	0.56	0.55	0.56	0.20
32	Manufacturing	1.37	1.36	1.38	0.31
33	Manufacturing	1.10	1.09	1.10	0.47
42	Wholesale trade	0.72	0.71	0.72	0.58
44	Retail trade	0.78	0.77	0.78	0.59
45	Retail trade	0.69	0.68	0.69	0.41
48	Transportation and warehousing	0.48	0.47	0.48	0.28
49	Transportation and warehousing	0.66	0.65	0.66	0.36
51	Information	0.32	0.30	0.32	0.44
52	Finance and insurance	0.31	0.31	0.31	0.31
53	Real estate	0.64	0.63	0.64	0.77
54	Prof., sci., and tech. services	0.54	0.53	0.55	0.37
56	Admin. and waste management services	0.66	0.66	0.67	0.48
61	Educational services	0.46	0.46	0.46	0.29
62	Health care and social assistance	0.79	0.79	0.78	0.75
71	Arts and recreation	0.77	0.77	0.78	0.59
72	Accom. and food services	0.71	0.69	0.70	0.66
81	Other services (except public administration)	0.52	0.51	0.52	0.39

NOTES: The disparity ratios are ratios of utilization to availability (U/A). Utilization is measured as the number of contracts awarded to WOSBs divided by the number of contracts in that industry, using FPDS data from FY05. Availability is measured as the number of WOSBs divided by the number of all firms in that industry, using 2006 CCR data. Ratios between 0.0 and 0.5 are highlighted in dark gray, and those between 0.5 and 0.8 are highlighted in light gray. Industries listed are those for which our power calculations indicated there were enough data to detect a small effect and the FPDS contained contracts. For more information about the power tests, see Appendix A.

one transportation subsector (48), information, finance, and educational services. WOSBs appear to be at least underrepresented in one manufacturing subsector (31), one retail trade subsector (45), one transportation subsector (49), professional services, administrative services, and other services.

In contrast, Table 4.4 shows that disparity ratios based on contract dollars indicate no underrepresentation.

The 2002 SBA report calculated a disparity ratio at the 2-digit industry-code level, but the NRC review suggested also estimating ratios at a more disaggregated level. RAND estimated disparity ratios similar to those presented in Tables 4.3 and 4.4 but at the 3- and 4-digit industry-code level where sample size allowed.[2] We found that there were industries at this level with few WOSBs. We used power calculations (described in Appendix A) to determine

[2] The broader definition of availability is measured using the SBO, which publishes data only at the 2-digit level.

Table 4.4
Disparity Ratios Using Contract Dollars and a Narrow Definition of Availability

		All Contracts		Trimmed Sample	
2-Digit Code	Industry	FPDS	FPDS and DUNS	FPDS	FPDS and DUNS
11	Forestry, fishing	43.95	43.95	54.12	54.12
21	Mining	89.81	89.77	101.7	101.7
22	Utilities	8.80	8.78	12.46	12.44
23	Construction	15.22	15.06	25.73	25.39
31	Manufacturing	2.34	2.34	2.83	2.82
32	Manufacturing	34.20	33.78	66.01	65.19
33	Manufacturing	7.53	7.10	33.81	33.10
42	Wholesale trade	29.69	29.39	19.80	19.46
44	Retail trade	52.88	50.10	88.01	83.43
45	Retail trade	41.86	40.63	50.68	49.18
48	Transportation and warehousing	9.30	9.12	18.11	17.66
49	Transportation and warehousing	146.0	145.0	260.7	259.0
51	Information	14.02	13.91	34.61	34.34
52	Finance and insurance	284.4	76.53	156.5	156.5
53	Real estate	73.58	72.53	51.98	49.69
54	Prof., sci., and tech. services	18.52	16.77	48.32	46.49
56	Admin. and waste management services	2.65	2.58	11.51	11.12
61	Educational services	7.27	7.19	21.59	21.36
62	Health care and social assistance	21.88	21.88	36.34	36.34
71	Arts and recreation	93.14	93.05	135.1	135.0
72	Accom. and food services	165.4	158.4	150.8	139.7
81	Other services (except public administration)	6.66	6.43	14.92	14.42

NOTE: The disparity ratios are ratios of utilization to availability (U/A). Utilization is measured as the contract dollars awarded to WOSBs divided by the total contract dollars in that industry, using FPDS data from FY05. Availability is measured as the total revenue of WOSBs divided by the revenue of all firms in that industry, using 2006 CCR data. Industries listed are those for which our power calculations indicated there were enough data to detect a small effect and the FPDS contained contracts. For more information about the power tests, see Appendix A.

which 3- and 4-digit industries had enough observations in the CCR to be able to detect small mean differences between WOSBs and other firms. On the basis of the results of the power test, we suppressed ratios for which we had insufficient samples. Given the number of ratios we estimated, we would expect to find at least several industries in which underrepresentation occurs just by chance, and we do.

As was the case in the 2-digit analysis, many more industries give evidence of underrepresentation when disparity is measured using number of contracts awarded rather than contract dollars awarded. Only five industries showed underrepresentation of WOSBs when we used the disparity ratios based on contract dollars. These are shown in Table 4.5; the full set of results, indicating the many industries that suggest underrepresentation when number of contracts is used to define disparity ratios, is given in Appendix B. Results were similar across the FPDS and DUNS definitions of small, so we present results using only the FPDS definition of small in order to combine the full- and trimmed-sample results in one table for easy reference.

Table 4.5
Industries in Which WOSBs Are Underrepresented When Disparity Ratios Are Defined Using Contract Dollars

	Disparity Ratio			
	Number of Contracts		Contract Dollars	
Industry Code	Full Sample	Trimmed Sample	Full Sample	Trimmed Sample
928	0.17	0.18	0.66	1.24
3328	0.55	0.54	0.50	2.25
3371	0.39	0.39	0.66	1.54
4412	0.85	0.84	0.34	0.58
9281	0.17	0.18	0.66	1.24

NOTE: The industries shown are the only ones in which the ratios measured using contract dollars fell into the underrepresentation range. The full set of industries appears in Appendix B. The ratios are measured as the ratio of utilization to availability (U/A). Utilization is measured as the number of contracts (dollars in contracts) awarded to WOSBs divided by the number of contracts (dollars) in that industry, using FPDS data from FY05. Availability is measured as the number (revenue) of WOSBs divided by the number of all firms (revenue) in that industry, using 2006 CCR data. Ratios between 0.0 and 0.5 are highlighted in dark gray, and those between 0.5 and 0.8 are highlighted in light gray. Industries listed are those for which our power calculations indicated there were enough data to detect a small effect and the FPDS contained contracts. For more information about the power tests, see Appendix A.

Table 4.6 summarizes how conclusions about the underrepresentation of WOSBs in government contracting can vary depending on the measure used. The table presents the percentage of industries showing evidence of underrepresentation and substantial underrepresentation, by the various ways we measured disparity. The percentages range from 0 to 87 percent.[3] For example, 55.6 percent of the 18 2-digit industries indicate underepresentation of WOSBs when disparity is measured using number of contracts and number of firms.

Our findings suggest that there is considerable sensitivity to the method of measurement of disparity ratios. When ratios are constructed based on number of contracts relative to the number of firms, it appears that WOSBs receive fewer government procurement contracts than their prevalence indicates should be the case in many industries. When ratios are constructed using contract dollars relative to firms' gross receipts, the outcome is considerably more variable, with WOSBs underrepresented in from 0 to 87 percent of industries.

Which measure is appropriate depends on the policy it is intended to support. Another consideration is the frequency with which these measures need to be updated. The SBO data from the Economic Census are available every five years. The CCR file is updated continuously as firms enter their names to the list of possible bidders. This means that the CCR is generally more current than the SBO, but it also means that the comparison group could change from month to month. In practice, this change may not be large, but this should be confirmed. Finally, the public-use SBO file is published at only the 2-digit industry level, and WOSBs

[3] Appendix B provides a similar table that indicates the percentage of federal government spending (as recorded in the FPDS) in industries in which WOSBs are underrepresented. This is not spending that would automatically go to WOSBs under the proposed policy because that policy applies only to contracts of less than $3 million ($5 million in manufacturing) and is applied only at the contracting officer's discretion. Nonetheless, it is an indication of whether there is significant spending in designated industries.

Table 4.6
Industries Showing Underrepresentation by Various Measures of Disparity

Availability Measure	Utilization Measure	Definition of Small	Contract Sample	Total Number of Industries	Percent of Industries
		2-Digit Industry Codes			
SBO employer firms	Number of contracts	FPDS	Full	18	55.6
SBO employer firms	Number of contracts	FPDS, DUNS	Full	18	55.6
SBO employer firms	Number of contracts	FPDS	Trimmed	18	72.2
SBO employer firms	Number of contracts	FPDS, DUNS	Trimmed	18	72.2
SBO employer firms	Contract dollars	FPDS	Full	18	55.6
SBO employer firms	Contract dollars	FPDS, DUNS	Full	18	55.6
SBO employer firms	Contract dollars	FPDS	Trimmed	18	27.8
SBO employer firms	Contract dollars	FPDS, DUNS	Trimmed	18	38.9
CCR registrants	Number of contracts	FPDS	Full	23	82.6
CCR registrants	Number of contracts	FPDS, DUNS	Full	23	82.6
CCR registrants	Number of contracts	FPDS	Trimmed	23	82.6
CCR registrants	Number of contracts	FPDS, DUNS	Trimmed	23	87.0
CCR registrants	Contract dollars	FPDS	Full	23	0.0
CCR registrants	Contract dollars	FPDS, DUNS	Full	23	0.0
CCR registrants	Contract dollars	FPDS	Trimmed	23	0.0
CCR registrants	Contract dollars	FPDS, DUNS	Trimmed	23	0.0
		3-Digit Industry Codes			
CCR registrants	Number of contracts	FPDS	Full	66	69.7
CCR registrants	Number of contracts	FPDS, DUNS	Full	66	69.7
CCR registrants	Number of contracts	FPDS	Trimmed	66	69.7
CCR registrants	Number of contracts	FPDS, DUNS	Trimmed	66	69.7
CCR registrants	Contract dollars	FPDS	Full	66	1.5
CCR registrants	Contract dollars	FPDS, DUNS	Full	66	1.5
CCR registrants	Contract dollars	FPDS	Trimmed	66	0.0
CCR registrants	Contract dollars	FPDS, DUNS	Trimmed	66	0.0
		4-Digit Industry Codes			
CCR registrants	Number of contracts	FPDS	Full	140	77.1
CCR registrants	Number of contracts	FPDS	Trimmed	140	77.1
CCR registrants	Contract dollars	FPDS	Full	140	2.9
CCR registrants	Contract dollars	FPDS	Trimmed	140	0.0

cannot be isolated from WOBs generally. The SBA could apply to the Census Bureau for access to the restricted underlying firm-level data in order to construct more-precise disparity ratios.

CHAPTER FIVE

Conclusion

Disparity ratios are used to measure differences in outcomes between groups. In this report, they are used to measure the representation of WOSBs versus other businesses in government contracting. Disparity ratios consist of two parts: (1) utilization, measured by government spending going to a category of firms (e.g., WOSBs) as a fraction of total procurement spending, and (2) the availability of such firms as a fraction of all firms. A disparity ratio is thus the ratio of utilization to availability. A disparity ratio equal to 1 means that government spending is approximately in line with the representation of particular firms in the economy. A disparity ratio of less than 1 suggests that these firms are underrepresented in government spending.

We tested different ways to measure utilization and availability, as requested by the SBA. Government contracting as recorded in the FPDS was used to measure utilization. One main area of testing was the comparison of ratios computed using number of contracts and number of firms with ratios computed using the dollar amount of contracts and the gross revenue of firms. In the former, the utilization of WOSBs was measured by comparing the number of contracts going to WOSBs as a fraction of all contracts, and availability was measured by comparing the number of WOSBs to the number of all firms. In contrast, the second set of ratios used dollar values. Utilization of WOSBs was measured by comparing the total contract dollars going to WOSBs as a fraction of all spending, and availability was measured by comparing total gross revenue of WOSBs to total gross revenue of all firms. Which method is most appropriate is a policy decision, not a research-driven one. Our goal was simply to show how conclusions about the representation of WOSBs in government procurement differ depending on the measure used. We found more evidence of underrepresentation when the measure is numbers of contracts than when the measure is contract dollars.

The other main area of testing was the measurement of availability. The goal, based on court decisions, was to measure availability among the pool of ready, willing, and able firms. There is some debate about how to measure this, and we used two different datasets to measure the pool of firms. In the first, all firms in the economy with at least one employee constitute the pool of ready, willing, and able firms. We used the 2002 SBO to identify these firms. In the second, the pool is defined as firms that have registered with the government as potential contractors. We used an October 2006 CCR file to identify these firms.

Data limitations drive these calculations. Because interviewing all firms would be enormously expensive, we had to rely on extant data. The SBO includes all firms. Firms that believe the government discriminates against them are probably less likely to register to bid on contracts. If that is the case, this broader definition of ready, willing, and able can be appropriate even though just how willing firms are is unknown. The SBO, however, identifies industries at only the 2-digit industry-code level, and it is conducted only every five years. More important, it does not publish data on WOSBs, but only on WOBs, which has the effect of biasing the disparity ratios downward (i.e., in favor of finding underrepresentation). It is possible that the SBA could apply to the Census Bureau for special runs on the microdata that could provide data at the 3- or 4-digit level and could identify WOSBs. These data are restricted for confidentiality reasons, and some expense and time delays could be incurred in obtaining them.

The CCR also has its strengths and weaknesses. Bidder lists have been used in prior studies of disparity to define ready, willing, and able firms. The willingness of firms is evidenced by their registration, but as with the SBO data, we are unable to confirm that a firm is ready and able. All but one firm in our file had at least one employee, our proxy for "able"; the only firms we deleted from the sample had erroneously large employment or revenue entries. The CCR data are also available at the 3- and 4-digit industry-code level, the database is updated continuously, and WOSBs can be identified. Unlike the SBO, however, the CCR does not include firms that have been discouraged from applying for government contracts.

The results vary considerably by whether the SBO or the CCR is used to define the pool of available firms. Using the SBO, we find that WOSBs are underrepresented in 56 to 72 percent of industries when the disparity ratios are based on number of contracts, and 28 to 56 percent of industries when disparity is based on contract dollars. (The exact percentage depends on the particular measure used; we also experimented with defining small firms by using DUNS data and by trimming very large and very small contracts from the FPDS data.) Using the CCR at the 2-digit level, we find that WOSBs are underrepresented in 83 to 87 percent of industries when disparity is measured using number of contracts and 0 percent of industries when it is measured using contract dollars. We were also able to disaggregate industries by their 3- and 4-digit NAICS codes in the CCR, with similar results. That disparity ratios vary so widely depending on the type of measurement used suggests that government contracts account for a larger share of total firm gross revenue for WOSBs than they do for other firms.

Finally, we note that disparity ratios are not in and of themselves measures of discrimination, although they have been used in numerous court cases to infer discrimination. Nonetheless, they are a starting point, a way to identify whether there are differences in outcomes between different types of firms. This report has provided a variety of ways to measure those differences.

Power Calculations

Women-owned small businesses appear to be underrepresented in a number of industries, particularly when the data are analyzed by 3- or 4-digit NAICS codes. We did not report disparity ratios for industries whose samples were too small to accurately calculate the ratios and credibly identify significant differences across groups. We were concerned that conclusions based on small samples may be influenced by chance and thus may not accurately capture true representation. For example, in an industry in which there are only four WOSBs and two contracts (0.5 contracts each) in a particular year, WOSBs may appear to be underrepresented if non-WOSB firms average one contract each. But the consistency of the disparity ratio may be quite low across years because an additional contract award or two may be won by chance and may eliminate the perceived underrepresentation. In this appendix, we describe the decision rule for determining which utilization measures to report.

The SBA is interested in whether the disparity ratios described above (D) are equal to 1 for each industry. This is equivalent to a test of whether the WOSB measure (numerator) is equal to the measure for all other businesses (denominator).

$$D = U/A = 1 \quad (1)$$

Because $U = C_W/C_T$ and $A = W/T$, we can rearrange the condition $D = 1$, as follows:

$$[C_W/C_T]/[W/T] = 1 \quad (2)$$

$$C_W/W = C_T/T \quad (3)$$

Equation 3 indicates that for the ratio to equal 1, the average number of contracts for each WOSB must be equal to the average number of contracts for all businesses, and by definition, to the number of contracts that go to non-WOSBs (NW).

$$C_W/W = C_T/T = [C_W + C_{NW}]/[W+NW] \quad (4)$$

$$C_W/W = C_{NW}/NW \quad (5)$$

We calculated power tests for two-sample equality of means for each 2-, 3-, and 4-digit NAICS industry to determine which ones had a sufficient number of firms in each group to identify a small difference between groups.

First, we determined the number of businesses in each sample for each NAICS industry, specifically, the number of WOSBs and the number of other businesses. We then used these sample sizes to calculate the smallest mean effect size that we could identify with a significance level of 0.05 and power 0.80.

In effect, our test examines whether there is a significant mean difference between the utilization of WOSBs and that of other businesses. The mean effect size is the difference between the two measures when they are standardized so that their standard deviation is equal to 1. In the social science literature, a mean effect size of 0.2 standard deviations is considered "small," 0.5 standard deviations is considered "medium," and 0.8 standard deviations is considered "large." Any NAICS for which we could not credibly identify an effect size of 0.2 was not reported.

Table A.1 shows the numbers of 2-, 3-, and 4-digit NAICS industry codes for which we can identify small, medium, and large differences using sample sizes from the CCR and SBO data.[1] The CCR contains sufficient observations to identify a small difference for all 2-digit NAICS codes except NAICS 55 (management of companies and enterprises), for 66 percent of the 3-digit NAICS codes, and for 44 percent of the 4-digit NAICS codes. The corresponding shares for a medium-size effect are 100 percent of 2-digit NAICS codes, 94 percent of 3-digit NAICS codes, and 85 percent of 4-digit NAICS codes. Large effects can be identified for all 2-digit NAICS codes and for nearly all 3- and 4-digit NAICS codes. Using the SBO data, we can identify a small effect for all 2-digit NAICS codes.

Table A.1
Results of Power Tests

	Small Effect (percent)	Medium Effect (percent)	Large Effect (percent)	Number of NAICS Industries
CCR data				
2-digit codes	95.8	100.0	100.0	24
3-digit codes	66.0	94.0	98.0	100
4-digit codes	44.2	85.2	94.6	317
SBO data				
2-digit codes	100.0	100.0	100.0	20

[1] This is the full sample from the CCR (no trims), using the FPDS definition of WOSBs.

Full Results

Table B.1
Disparity Ratios Based on Contract Dollars by Year, Using the Full FPDS and All Employer Firms as a Comparison Group

	FY 02		FY 03		Both Years Combined	
Industry Code	Small Defined by FPDS	Small Defined by FPDS and DUNS	Small Defined by FPDS	Small Defined by FPDS and DUNS	Small Defined by FPDS	Small Defined by FPDS and DUNS
11	0.73	0.72	1.33	1.33	1.13	1.13
21	0.99	0.95	10.12	10.06	6.07	6.02
22	6.26	6.14	7.97	7.77	7.30	7.13
23	0.96	0.93	1.05	1.02	1.02	0.99
31	0.67	0.62	0.61	0.56	0.63	0.58
42	0.65	0.57	0.37	0.35	0.48	0.43
44	1.13	1.09	0.94	0.87	1.01	0.95
48	0.17	0.18	0.19	0.18	0.18	0.18
51	2.37	2.02	1.65	1.61	1.97	1.79
52	0.18	0.15	0.14	0.08	0.15	0.10
53	0.69	0.68	1.33	1.32	1.02	1.01
54	0.48	0.37	0.50	0.41	0.49	0.39
56	0.38	0.36	0.40	0.39	0.39	0.38
61	0.71	0.51	0.26	0.25	0.38	0.32
62	1.49	1.47	1.15	1.13	1.26	1.24
71	0.83	0.83	1.28	1.28	1.05	1.04
72	1.47	1.38	0.93	0.92	1.16	1.12
81	0.26	0.25	0.24	0.23	0.24	0.23

NOTE: The disparity ratios are ratios of utilization to availability (U/A). Utilization is measured as the contract dollars awarded to WOSBs divided by the total contract dollars awarded in that industry, using FPDS data from FY02 and FY03. Availability is measured as the total receipts of women-owned employer firms divided by the total receipts of all employer firms in that industry, using 2002 SBO data. Industries listed are those for which our power calculations indicated there were enough data to detect a small effect and the FPDS contained contracts. For more information about the power tests, see Appendix A.

Table B.2
Disparity Ratios Based on Number of Contracts by Year, Using the Full FPDS and All Employer Firms as a Comparison Group

	FY 02		FY 03		Both Years Combined	
Industry Code	Small Defined by FPDS	Small Defined by FPDS and DUNS	Small Defined by FPDS	Small Defined by FPDS and DUNS	Small Defined by FPDS	Small Defined by FPDS and DUNS
11	0.92	0.91	0.98	0.98	0.96	0.95
21	0.85	0.82	0.80	0.79	0.82	0.80
22	0.47	0.45	0.37	0.36	0.40	0.39
23	1.53	1.49	1.57	1.54	1.55	1.52
31	0.50	0.48	0.71	0.69	0.64	0.63
42	0.90	0.86	0.91	0.89	0.91	0.88
44	0.58	0.55	0.55	0.53	0.56	0.54
48	0.49	0.48	0.45	0.44	0.46	0.45
51	0.49	0.47	0.52	0.49	0.51	0.48
52	0.26	0.23	0.17	0.14	0.21	0.18
53	0.19	0.18	0.20	0.19	0.19	0.19
54	0.45	0.42	0.50	0.48	0.48	0.46
56	0.72	0.69	0.72	0.70	0.72	0.70
61	0.31	0.31	0.35	0.35	0.34	0.33
62	0.47	0.46	0.57	0.56	0.52	0.51
71	1.66	1.64	1.76	1.74	1.73	1.72
72	0.48	0.46	0.47	0.45	0.47	0.45
81	0.27	0.26	0.32	0.30	0.30	0.29

NOTE: The disparity ratios are ratios of utilization to availability (U/A). Utilization is measured as the number of contracts awarded to WOSBs divided by the number of contracts in that industry, using FPDS data from FY02 and FY03. Availability is measured as the number of women-owned employer firms divided by the number of all employer firms in that industry, using 2002 SBO data. Industries listed are those for which our power calculations indicated there were enough data to detect a small effect and the FPDS contained contracts. For more information about the power tests, see Appendix A.

Table B.3
Disparity Ratios Based on Contract Dollars by Year, Using the Trimmed FPDS and All Employer Firms as a Comparison Group

	FY 02		FY 03		Both Years Combined	
Industry Code	Small Defined by FPDS	Small Defined by FPDS and DUNS	Small Defined by FPDS	Small Defined by FPDS and DUNS	Small Defined by FPDS	Small Defined by FPDS and DUNS
11	0.75	0.74	1.33	1.33	1.14	1.13
21	0.96	0.92	11.49	11.42	6.41	6.35
22	7.85	7.70	9.52	9.27	8.88	8.68
23	1.24	1.20	1.48	1.44	1.38	1.34
31	1.33	1.22	1.59	1.51	1.48	1.39
42	1.07	0.94	0.87	0.81	0.96	0.87
44	2.73	2.64	2.39	2.22	2.51	2.37
48	0.42	0.41	0.45	0.44	0.44	0.43
51	3.30	3.21	3.24	3.16	3.27	3.19
52	1.73	1.50	3.13	1.78	2.59	1.67
53	0.52	0.51	0.70	0.69	0.61	0.60
54	0.81	0.69	0.92	0.79	0.87	0.75
56	0.74	0.70	0.87	0.84	0.81	0.78
61	1.06	0.76	0.71	0.67	0.85	0.71
62	1.60	1.58	1.68	1.66	1.65	1.63
71	1.15	1.15	1.65	1.65	1.40	1.39
72	2.48	2.33	1.21	1.19	1.68	1.61
81	0.36	0.35	0.47	0.45	0.42	0.41

NOTE: The disparity ratios are ratios of utilization to availability (U/A). Utilization is measured as the contract dollars awarded to WOSBs divided by the total contract dollars awarded in that industry, using FPDS data from FY02 and FY03 trimmed of the largest and smallest 0.5 percent of contracts. Availability is measured as the total receipts of women-owned employer firms divided by the total receipts of all employer firms in that industry, using 2002 SBO data. Industries listed are those for which our power calculations indicated there were enough data to detect a small effect and the FPDS contained contracts. For more information about the power tests, see Appendix A.

Table B.4
Disparity Ratios Based on Number of Contracts by Year, Using the Trimmed FPDS and All Employer Firms as a Comparison Group

	FY 02		FY 03		Both Years Combined	
Industry Code	Small Defined by FPDS	Small Defined by FPDS and DUNS	Small Defined by FPDS	Small Defined by FPDS and and DUNS	Small Defined by FPDS	Small Defined by FPDS and DUNS
11	0.92	0.90	0.98	0.98	0.96	0.95
21	0.86	0.83	0.81	0.80	0.83	0.81
22	0.47	0.45	0.37	0.36	0.40	0.39
23	1.53	1.50	1.58	1.55	1.56	1.53
31	0.51	0.49	0.71	0.70	0.65	0.63
42	0.90	0.87	0.91	0.90	0.91	0.88
44	0.58	0.56	0.55	0.53	0.56	0.54
48	0.49	0.48	0.46	0.44	0.47	0.46
51	0.49	0.47	0.52	0.49	0.51	0.48
52	0.28	0.24	0.18	0.15	0.22	0.19
53	0.19	0.18	0.19	0.19	0.19	0.19
54	0.45	0.43	0.51	0.49	0.48	0.46
56	0.72	0.70	0.73	0.71	0.72	0.70
61	0.31	0.31	0.35	0.35	0.34	0.34
62	0.47	0.46	0.57	0.56	0.52	0.51
71	1.66	1.64	1.77	1.75	1.74	1.72
72	0.48	0.45	0.47	0.45	0.47	0.45
81	0.27	0.26	0.32	0.31	0.30	0.29

NOTE: The disparity ratios are ratios of utilization to availability (U/A). Utilization is measured as the number of contracts to WOSBs divided by the number of contracts in that industry, using FPDS data from FY02 and FY03 trimmed of the largest and smallest 0.5 percent of contracts. Availability is measured as the number of women-owned employer firms divided by the number of all employer firms in that industry, using 2002 SBO data. Industries listed are those for which our power calculations indicated there were enough data to detect a small effect and the FPDS contained contracts. For more information about the power tests, see Appendix A.

Table B.5
Disparity Ratios at the 3-Digit Industry-Code Level, Based on Contract Dollars, Using Firms Registered in the CCR as a Comparison Group

	Full Sample		Trimmed Sample	
Industry Code	Small Defined by FPDS	Small Defined by FPDS and DUNS	Small Defined by FPDS	Small Defined by FPDS and DUNS
113	104.67	104.67	103.98	103.98
115	16.34	16.34	16.34	16.34
221	8.70	8.68	12.49	12.47
236	13.96	13.79	30.03	29.51
237	19.51	19.23	31.04	30.60
238	31.27	31.13	28.16	27.99
311	0.83	0.83	0.88	0.88
314	6.12	6.08	6.65	6.58
315	2.70	2.70	3.77	3.77
321	17.36	17.25	17.35	17.24
322	5.26	5.24	6.67	6.64
323	1.88	1.82	18.44	17.84
325	49.73	49.44	96.01	95.47
326	9.01	8.76	11.26	10.94
327	12.91	12.86	12.42	12.38
331	3.30	3.28	5.56	5.53
332	4.41	4.34	12.57	12.38
333	20.50	15.92	25.81	24.94
334	6.51	5.78	17.86	17.09
335	31.04	30.84	35.01	34.78
336	3.35	3.31	25.77	25.32
337	2.05	2.00	3.04	2.97
339	5.28	5.23	6.99	6.92
423	41.58	41.21	23.60	23.16
424	7.37	7.25	7.97	7.85
425	148.21	148.21	148.21	148.21
441	2.38	2.38	3.68	3.68
442	6.03	5.99	6.02	5.98
443	6.54	5.98	9.80	8.97
444	631.56	630.61	612.74	611.81
446	0.83	0.82	5.47	5.47
448	5.77	5.77	5.77	5.77
451	399.72	399.72	1024.40	1024.40
453	22.56	22.32	22.52	22.28
454	6.33	5.34	6.31	5.33
484	8.88	8.88	14.78	14.77
485	18.46	18.39	18.47	18.41
488	8.11	7.72	15.30	13.84
492	69.76	69.27	69.76	69.27

Table B.5 (continued)

	Full Sample		Trimmed Sample	
Industry Code	Small Defined by FPDS	Small Defined by FPDS and DUNS	Small Defined by FPDS	Small Defined by FPDS and DUNS
493	6.10	6.05	12.36	12.26
511	27.73	27.31	27.66	27.25
512	30.16	30.06	40.55	40.42
516	44.74	41.98	44.66	41.92
517	5.16	5.11	20.32	20.16
518	19.54	19.44	38.41	38.21
519	16.30	16.27	43.09	42.99
524	179.75	179.75	329.03	329.03
531	374.74	374.49	175.46	174.29
532	10.60	9.38	24.82	21.97
541	18.58	16.88	48.03	46.33
561	2.68	2.62	11.42	11.10
562	3.80	3.47	22.30	20.38
611	7.20	7.20	21.43	21.42
621	18.92	18.92	33.49	33.49
624	11.19	11.19	25.32	25.32
711	9.17	9.15	9.13	9.12
713	122.17	122.17	279.74	279.74
721	172.62	156.96	175.57	160.24
722	59.54	57.37	61.23	56.95
811	4.84	4.78	12.35	12.20
812	42.18	34.45	53.97	44.40
813	68.66	68.66	68.12	68.12
921	6.51	6.51	35.20	35.20
922	2.70	2.70	15.69	15.69
923	19.63	19.63	19.61	19.61
928	0.66	0.66	1.24	1.24

NOTE: The disparity ratios are ratios of utilization to availability (U/A). Utilization is measured as the contract dollars awarded to WOSBs divided by the contract dollars awarded in that industry, using FPDS data from FY05. Availability is measured as the gross revenue of WOSBs divided by the gross revenue of all firms in that industry, using 2006 CCR data. Industries listed are those for which our power calculations indicated there were enough data to detect a small effect and the FPDS contained contracts. For more information about the power tests, see Appendix A.

Table B.6
Disparity Ratios at the 3-Digit Industry-Code Level, Based on Number of Contracts, Using Firms Registered in the CCR as a Comparison Group

	Full Sample		Trimmed Sample	
Industry Code	Small Defined by FPDS	Small Defined by FPDS and DUNS	Small Defined by FPDS	Small Defined by FPDS and DUNS
113	0.67	0.67	0.67	0.67
115	0.90	0.89	0.89	0.89
221	0.34	0.33	0.34	0.33
236	0.89	0.87	0.91	0.90
237	0.74	0.74	0.75	0.75
238	0.71	0.70	0.71	0.70
311	0.48	0.48	0.48	0.48
314	0.57	0.55	0.57	0.56
315	0.51	0.51	0.51	0.51
321	0.67	0.66	0.67	0.66
322	0.56	0.53	0.56	0.53
323	0.34	0.33	0.34	0.33
325	1.91	1.90	1.91	1.90
326	0.56	0.53	0.56	0.53
327	3.18	3.17	3.18	3.17
331	1.12	1.11	1.12	1.11
332	1.16	1.16	1.16	1.16
333	1.24	1.22	1.24	1.22
334	0.79	0.77	0.80	0.77
335	1.30	1.29	1.30	1.29
336	0.95	0.94	0.96	0.95
337	0.47	0.46	0.47	0.46
339	1.02	1.01	1.02	1.01
423	0.74	0.72	0.74	0.72
424	0.57	0.56	0.56	0.56
425	0.87	0.87	0.87	0.87
441	0.83	0.83	0.83	0.82
442	0.48	0.47	0.48	0.47
443	0.70	0.67	0.70	0.67
444	1.32	1.32	1.33	1.32
446	0.36	0.35	0.36	0.35
448	0.38	0.38	0.38	0.38
451	0.97	0.97	0.97	0.97
453	0.68	0.67	0.68	0.67
454	0.38	0.37	0.38	0.37
484	0.58	0.58	0.58	0.58
485	0.58	0.54	0.58	0.54
488	0.45	0.43	0.45	0.43
492	0.75	0.74	0.75	0.74
493	0.46	0.45	0.46	0.45

Table B.6 (continued)

	Full Sample		Trimmed Sample	
Industry Code	**Small Defined by FPDS**	**Small Defined by FPDS and DUNS**	**Small Defined by FPDS**	**Small Defined by FPDS and DUNS**
511	0.35	0.33	0.35	0.33
512	0.67	0.64	0.67	0.64
516	0.21	0.17	0.21	0.18
517	0.26	0.24	0.26	0.24
518	0.37	0.35	0.37	0.36
519	0.38	0.37	0.38	0.37
524	0.23	0.23	0.23	0.23
531	0.99	0.98	0.98	0.98
532	0.37	0.37	0.37	0.37
541	0.54	0.53	0.55	0.54
561	0.67	0.67	0.68	0.67
562	0.60	0.58	0.60	0.59
611	0.46	0.46	0.46	0.46
621	0.76	0.76	0.76	0.76
624	0.92	0.92	0.92	0.92
711	0.81	0.81	0.81	0.81
713	0.82	0.82	0.83	0.83
721	0.74	0.72	0.74	0.72
722	0.66	0.66	0.66	0.65
811	0.49	0.48	0.49	0.48
812	0.34	0.33	0.34	0.32
813	0.90	0.90	0.90	0.90
921	0.60	0.60	0.60	0.60
922	0.87	0.87	0.87	0.87
923	0.29	0.29	0.29	0.29
928	0.17	0.17	0.18	0.18

NOTE: The disparity ratios are ratios of utilization to availability (U/A). Utilization is measured as the number of contracts awarded to WOSBs divided by the number of contracts awarded in that industry, using FPDS data from FY05. Availability is measured as the number of WOSBs divided by the number of all firms in that industry, using 2006 CCR data. Industries listed are those for which our power calculations indicated there were enough data to detect a small effect and the FPDS contained contracts. For more information about the power tests, see Appendix A.

Table B.7
Disparity Ratios at the 4-Digit Industry-Code Level, Using Firms Registered in the CCR as a Comparison Group

	Outcome Measure			
	Number of Contracts		Contract Dollars	
Industry Code	Full Sample	Trimmed Sample	Full Sample	Trimmed Sample
1153	0.87	0.87	4.81	4.81
2213	0.51	0.51	65.02	76.92
2361	0.52	0.52	3.02	14.03
2362	0.94	0.96	13.51	28.22
2371	0.66	0.66	19.74	26.20
2372	0.17	0.17	4.30	4.30
2373	0.87	0.88	18.21	25.65
2379	0.83	0.85	25.78	45.63
2381	0.65	0.64	31.16	16.51
2382	0.72	0.72	43.81	43.55
2383	0.56	0.57	19.47	19.38
2389	0.70	0.70	20.77	26.20
3149	0.63	0.63	6.69	7.35
3152	0.45	0.45	1.63	2.42
3159	0.61	0.61	14.93	18.75
3219	0.66	0.66	13.93	13.92
3222	0.56	0.56	3.75	4.36
3231	0.34	0.34	1.88	18.39
3259	0.40	0.41	2.95	4.81
3321	0.72	0.72	10.27	10.26
3323	0.71	0.71	3.62	8.64
3324	0.63	0.63	2.93	13.13
3327	0.88	0.88	2.01	2.27
3328	0.55	0.54	0.50	2.25
3329	0.50	0.50	3.37	11.39
3332	0.88	0.88	19.66	19.60
3333	0.58	0.58	95.89	120.15
3334	1.10	1.10	107.79	108.59
3335	0.88	0.87	12.64	14.47
3339	1.79	1.80	10.75	15.13
3341	0.92	0.92	37.47	68.83
3342	0.66	0.66	4.24	9.70
3344	0.89	0.89	22.64	42.78
3345	0.58	0.58	5.63	17.96
3346	0.58	0.59	22.81	44.12
3353	0.76	0.76	17.56	21.64
3359	0.78	0.78	23.40	25.20
3363	0.87	0.88	5.74	27.90
3364	1.00	1.01	2.77	25.52
3369	0.76	0.77	10.50	78.29
3371	0.39	0.39	0.66	1.54
3372	0.50	0.50	3.62	3.78

Table B.7 (continued)

	Outcome Measure			
	Number of Contracts		Contract Dollars	
Industry Code	Full Sample	Trimmed Sample	Full Sample	Trimmed Sample
3391	0.32	0.32	13.34	16.48
3399	1.27	1.27	4.48	6.04
4231	0.63	0.63	10.87	10.87
4232	0.57	0.57	4.74	4.72
4233	0.69	0.69	6.75	6.74
4234	0.58	0.58	20.00	9.69
4236	0.61	0.61	18.89	18.70
4237	0.89	0.89	180.39	182.27
4238	0.89	0.89	12.87	18.62
4239	0.41	0.41	12.20	12.19
4241	0.36	0.36	9.80	9.94
4243	0.41	0.41	6.87	6.87
4244	1.08	1.07	26.60	26.66
4246	0.41	0.41	4.43	4.43
4248	0.47	0.47	4.68	4.68
4249	0.44	0.44	8.73	8.73
4251	0.87	0.87	147.00	147.00
4412	0.85	0.84	0.34	0.58
4413	0.95	0.95	5.59	5.59
4421	0.52	0.52	6.95	6.95
4422	0.39	0.39	3.34	3.32
4431	0.70	0.70	6.56	9.28
4441	1.37	1.37	675.59	673.59
4461	0.36	0.36	0.83	5.47
4511	0.68	0.69	2.03	6.82
4532	0.52	0.52	17.94	17.91
4539	0.90	0.90	38.55	38.49
4541	0.59	0.59	9.69	9.69
4543	0.37	0.37	6.56	6.54
4841	0.32	0.32	2.96	7.28
4842	0.70	0.71	9.84	9.82
4881	0.62	0.62	21.39	32.62
4884	0.58	0.57	11.34	11.47
4885	0.62	0.62	6.84	6.79
4889	0.33	0.32	3.25	5.59
4931	0.46	0.46	6.10	12.36
5111	0.28	0.28	23.95	23.95
5112	0.39	0.39	15.87	15.82
5121	0.68	0.68	39.85	55.27
5161	0.21	0.21	44.74	44.66
5171	0.22	0.22	2.01	11.37
5172	0.09	0.09	4.43	6.94
5173	0.48	0.48	10.14	23.59

Table B.7 (continued)

	Outcome Measure			
	Number of Contracts		Contract Dollars	
Industry Code	Full Sample	Trimmed Sample	Full Sample	Trimmed Sample
5179	0.29	0.29	14.03	49.85
5181	0.20	0.20	110.79	110.52
5182	0.49	0.50	12.16	23.86
5191	0.38	0.38	16.31	43.10
5311	0.62	0.59	725.58	312.91
5312	0.20	0.21	18.46	18.21
5313	0.89	0.88	104.35	106.51
5324	0.49	0.49	16.45	20.66
5411	0.48	0.49	6.27	12.34
5412	0.48	0.48	31.52	45.16
5413	0.60	0.62	13.40	38.26
5414	0.69	0.70	4.11	26.67
5415	0.57	0.57	40.87	74.12
5416	0.62	0.63	47.64	81.56
5417	0.41	0.41	16.12	42.63
5418	0.46	0.46	14.12	15.32
5419	0.54	0.54	8.32	29.70
5611	0.68	0.68	13.97	21.30
5612	0.64	0.66	2.98	29.58
5613	0.96	0.96	7.28	7.02
5614	0.74	0.75	19.58	86.61
5615	0.19	0.19	2.25	7.88
5616	0.73	0.73	29.64	42.75
5617	0.70	0.70	1.61	2.21
5619	0.37	0.38	3.18	8.58
5621	0.43	0.44	16.34	16.18
5622	0.45	0.46	7.49	44.54
5629	0.81	0.83	2.68	18.66
6114	0.48	0.49	8.28	9.85
6115	0.45	0.45	13.39	22.84
6116	0.55	0.55	3.18	3.28
6117	0.47	0.47	17.71	24.24
6211	0.91	0.89	41.82	46.67
6213	0.90	0.90	19.52	29.13
6214	0.53	0.52	1.40	18.76
6219	0.51	0.50	28.69	30.02
6241	1.59	1.60	7.03	25.79
6242	0.35	0.35	26.30	53.50
6243	0.50	0.50	10.92	10.90
7111	1.47	1.47	20.20	20.20
7115	0.56	0.56	1.12	1.11
7139	0.87	0.87	28.28	66.03
7211	0.42	0.41	122.42	127.15

Table B.7 (continued)

	Outcome Measure			
	Number of Contracts		Contract Dollars	
Industry Code	Full Sample	Trimmed Sample	Full Sample	Trimmed Sample
7212	1.33	1.33	55.08	55.08
7223	0.63	0.63	64.88	68.44
8111	0.79	0.79	8.43	19.05
8112	0.36	0.36	1.68	5.48
8113	0.55	0.55	37.27	40.22
8114	0.79	0.79	9.02	8.98
8129	0.25	0.25	20.16	24.79
8139	0.35	0.35	33.55	33.51
9211	0.60	0.60	6.51	35.20
9221	0.87	0.87	2.70	15.69
9231	0.29	0.29	19.48	19.47
9281	0.17	0.18	0.66	1.24

NOTE: The disparity ratios are ratios of utilization to availability (U/A). Utilization is measured as the number of contracts awarded to WOSBs divided by the number of contracts awarded in that industry, using FPDS data from FY05. Availability is measured as the number of WOSBs divided by the number of all firms in that industry, using 2006 CCR data. Industries listed are those for which our power calculations indicated there were enough data to detect a small effect and the FPDS contained contracts. For more information about the power tests, see Appendix A. The results with the FPDS and DUNS were similar, so we present the full- and trimmed-sample results in one table, using the FPDS definition of small.

Table B.8
Percentage of Government Spending in Industries Showing Underrepresentation by Various Measures of Disparity

Availability Measure	Utilization Measure	Definition of Small	Contract Sample	Total Number of Industries	Percentage of Government Spending
		2-Digit Industry Codes			
SBO employer firms	Number of contracts	FPDS	Full	18	85.7
SBO employer firms	Number of contracts	FPDS, DUNS	Full	18	85.7
SBO employer firms	Number of contracts	FPDS	Trimmed	18	84.2
SBO employer firms	Number of contracts	FPDS, DUNS	Trimmed	18	84.2
SBO employer firms	Contract dollars	FPDS	Full	18	85.7
SBO employer firms	Contract dollars	FPDS, DUNS	Full	18	85.7
SBO employer firms	Contract dollars	FPDS	Trimmed	18	15.1
SBO employer firms	Contract dollars	FPDS, DUNS	Trimmed	18	48.6
CCR registrants	Number of contracts	FPDS	Full	23	64.5
CCR registrants	Number of contracts	FPDS, DUNS	Full	23	64.5
CCR registrants	Number of contracts	FPDS	Trimmed	23	75.5
CCR registrants	Number of contracts	FPDS, DUNS	Trimmed	23	99.5
CCR registrants	Contract dollars	FPDS	Full	23	0.0
CCR registrants	Contract dollars	FPDS, DUNS	Full	23	0.0
CCR registrants	Contract dollars	FPDS	Trimmed	23	0.0
CCR registrants	Contract dollars	FPDS, DUNS	Trimmed	23	0.0
		3-Digit Industry Codes			
CCR registrants	Number of contracts	FPDS	Full	66	64.0
CCR registrants	Number of contracts	FPDS, DUNS	Full	66	64.0
CCR registrants	Number of contracts	FPDS	Trimmed	66	73.2
CCR registrants	Number of contracts	FPDS, DUNS	Trimmed	66	73.2
CCR registrants	Contract dollars	FPDS	Full	66	0.1
CCR registrants	Contract dollars	FPDS, DUNS	Full	66	0.1
CCR registrants	Contract dollars	FPDS	Trimmed	66	0.0
CCR registrants	Contract dollars	FPDS, DUNS	Trimmed	66	0.0
		4-Digit Industry Codes			
CCR registrants	Number of contracts	FPDS	Full	140	73.0
CCR registrants	Number of contracts	FPDS	Trimmed	140	79.3
CCR registrants	Contract dollars	FPDS	Full	140	3.4
CCR registrants	Contract dollars	FPDS	Trimmed	140	0.1

Bibliography

Dixon, Lloyd, Chad Shirley, Laura H. Baldwin, John A. Ausink, and Nancy F. Campbell, *An Assessment of Air Force Data on Contract Expenditures*, Santa Monica, CA: RAND Corporation, MG-274-AF, 2005.

Eagle Eye Publishers, Inc., *Analysis of Type of Business Coding for the Top 1,000 Contractors Receiving Small Business Awards in FY 2002*, Prepared for the SBA Office of Advocacy, Fairfax, VA: Eagle Eye Publishers, Inc., 2004.

Federal Procurement Data System, *Small Business Goaling Report 2005*. As of April 1, 2007: http://www.sba.gov/GC/goals/SmallBusinessGoalingReport_2005.pdf

Lowry, Ying, *Women in Business, 2006: A Demographic Review of Women's Business Ownership*, Washington, DC: Small Business Administration, Office of Advocacy, 2006. As of April 1, 2007: http://www.sba.gov/advo/research/rs280tot.pdf

National Research Council, *Analyzing Information on Women-Owned Small Businesses in Federal Contracting*, Steering Committee for the Workshop on Women-Owned Small Businesses in Federal Contracting, Committee on National Statistics, Division of Behavioral and Social Sciences and Education, Washington, DC: The National Academies Press, 2005.